Sacred Heart Catholic Church
The History: 1908-2008

Cover design: Pelican Ventures, LLC

ISBN-10 0-9712522-0-3
ISBN-13 978-0-9712522-0-2

Gloria Deo Books
an imprint of Pelican Ventures, LLC
P.O. Box 1738
Aztec NM 87410

Sacred Heart Catholic Church
The History: 1908-2008

Before 1900, the area along the San Juan River from what is now the Navajo Dam all the way to Waterflow was ministered to by priests from El Rito, Abiquiu, Rio Arriba, Tierra Amarilla and Durango. The priests ministering to these areas were for the most part diocesan priests of the Archdiocese of Santa Fe of which the San Juan Basin was a part before the formation of the Diocese of Gallup in 1939.

On April 28, 1900, Archbishop Peter Bourgade states "the part of the Archdiocese of Santa Fe known as San Juan County and Rio San Juan has been erected into a new mission or parish. The parish includes the settlements of Blanco, Largo, Pine River, Farmington, Aztec and La Plata."

In May 1900 Rev. Jean M. Garnier, a diocesan priest of the Archdiocese of Santa Fe, took residence in Largo and visited Farmington, according to the 1987 history written by Rev. Dacian Batt, O.F.M. ("A Brief History of Sacred Heart Parish, Farmington: 1905-1987"). Father Batt states that Sacred Heart Parish officially became a parish in 1908 when Father Garnier took up official residence in Farmington.

The first pastor of the widespread area was born December 26, 1856, in Cruet, France. Before coming to the United States of America, he studied at Petit Seminaire de Olbigny and Grand Seminaire de Chamberry. Then he arrived in the United States, going to Baltimore to study for one year at St. Mary's Seminary. He was ordained a Roman Catholic priest on March 4, 1882, by Archbishop John Baptist Lamy.

Archbishop Lamy was the first bishop of the Diocese of Santa Fe, consecrated on Nov. 24, 1850. Lamy later became archbishop when Santa Fe became an Archdiocese in 1875. Lamy is the famed central character of Willa Cather's novel "Death Comes to the Archbishop."

Father Garnier served as assistant in Santa Fe, then Tularosa and Lincoln City until 1887. In 1887, he was appointed to La Junta. From 1889 to 1894, he served at Mora. In 1890, he was appointed pastor. He succeeded Father Fourchegu as pastor in Mora. He was made chancellor and Cathedral assistant pastor in Santa Fe in 1894. This position was short-lived because a year later, in 1895, he was replaced as chancellor by Father Pouget. In 1898, Father Garnier was in Jemez. The archives lists Father Garnier at Blanco in 1910. Then March through June 1911, the archives list him as filling in for Father Haelterman in Santa Cruz. Father Garnier died on Dec. 23, 1912 as pastor of Costilla. He was only 56 years old when he died.

From the baptismal register held at Sacred heart Church, the first baptism in Farmington is recorded. It was on Sept. 25, 1900. The record states: "I have baptized Andrew Joseph born in Farmington, New Mexico, November the 1st, 1899, of Andrew Stevenson and Nellie Smith Stevenson. The sponsors were A. Laughlin Smith and Catherine Smith O'Leary." The record is signed "J.M. Garnier."

Some time around 1904, according to Father Dacian Batt's history, the headquarters of the San Juan County Parish was moved to Blanco. Father J.M. Garnier was still listed as the pastor of the entire area.

The railroad, which had been extended from Durango to Farmington in 1905, caused a major surge in activity in the small town, so much so that Father Garnier moved to Farmington three years later, in 1908, since there were more baptisms by that time than there were in Blanco. Father Garnier had quite a task in covering the parish of San Juan County: 16 missions attached to Farmington now and 10 other missions which were called the Blanco Missions. Some of the names of these missions were Blanco, Bloomfield, Aztec, Haynes, Turley, Archuleta, Los Martinez, Pine River, Canada, Bonita, Gobernador, Jaramillo, Francis, La Fragua and Ojo de Cueva.

In the early days of Father Garnier's time as pastor, there were already 1,326 children and adults listed as attending these missions.

According to an article in the Farmington Daily Times on June 8, 1984, the pastor would celebrate Masses in private homes until 1905 when the first Roman Catholic mission church was built in Farmington. This small structure was located on Pinon Street where Drake Well Servicing Company is now located.

In September 1910, the Franciscan Provincial in Cincinnati agreed to take over the San Juan County Parish. Father Albert Daeger, O.F.M., was the first Franciscan pastor of Sacred Heart Parish (1910 -

1916) and Father Marcellus Troester, O.F.M., was his first assistant rector in Farmington, according to the directories of St. John the Baptist and Our Lady of Guadalupe Provinces. Father Albert was born in St. Anne, Indiana, in 1872. He became a friar in the last class of novices to be invested at Oldenburg, Indiana, in 1889, and was ordained in 1896. He first assisted in Kansas City, Missouri, and Lincoln, Nebraska.

In 1902, he went to Pena Blanca, New Mexico, as pastor and superior. Following this assignment he was pastor at Farmington and then at Jemez. In 1919, Father Albert was appointed Archbishop of Santa Fe. He died suddenly on Dec. 2, 1932, after falling down a coal chute by accident in downtown Santa Fe. He died instantly and was deeply mourned.

Father Marcellus was born in Cincinnati, Ohio, in 1878. He was invested in 1898 and ordained in 1906, after which he was sent to St. Michaels, Arizona. His first major project was building a chapel at Lukachukai, Arizona. He also built the church at Tohatchi, New Mexico, living in a tent during the construction. Father Marcellus is credited with the opening of the mission territory to the north of St. Michaels, centering around Shiprock. He also began working with the Ute Indians in Colorado. Beginning in 1913, he helped edit and publish the annual "Franciscan Missions of the Southwest." In his later years, Father Marcellus undertook a census of the Navajo Tribe. At the time of his death, he was engaged in preparing a new edition of the Navajo catechism. He died Jan. 17, 1936, while chaplain at St. Michaels, after 30 years in the mission field. With a flair for languages and a lively curiosity, Father Marcellus can be regarded as the first to recognize the Navajos' special place in U.S. history and world ethnology.

Father Fintan came along with Father Theodore Stephan, O.F.M., to help Father Daeger, in 1912. Father Theodore was born in Cincinnati, Ohio, in 1862. He was invested at St. Clement, Cincinnati, in 1878, and ordained in 1885. The first 10 years of his priestly life were spent as excurrens from Bloomington, Illinois; Minonk, Illinois; and Emporia, Kansas, to the outlying missions. Later he was excurrens from St. Boniface, Lafayette, Indiana; to St. Lawrence, also in Lafayette. In 1901, he went to Pena Blanca as assistant, and four years later was appointed to Carlsbad, where he had charge of the Mexican missions. He returned to Pena Blanca and Jemez and died while stationed at Jemez on Oct. 30, 1918, after 33 years of priesthood.

Father Fintan, who became pastor of Sacred Heart in 1917 and remained in that position until 1932, was a native of Cincinnati, Ohio, born in 1879. He was invested in 1897. After ordination in 1905, he spent his entire career in the Southwestern missions, beginning with his first appointment to St. Michaels, Arizona, in 1905. For 15 years he was superior there. He was also superior at Farmington, except for one year when he was at St. Michaels as head of the missions to the Navajo. His last appointment was to Kansas City, Missouri, at Our Lady of Sorrows, where he lived in retirement. He died on Dec. 30, 1947, after 41 years in the missions.

By 1912 Father Fintan, in those early days, would take care of the growing parish in Farmington while the assistant pastor would be a

Father Fintan Zumbalen

circuit rider and ride horseback to make visits to outlying missions, which in 1912 totated 26.

The deed for the first church in Farmington at the time the diocesan priest built it reads: "In the year of our Lord 1905 a branch of railroad D.R. (broad guage) from Durango, Colorado, to Farmington, New Mexico, was built. Catholics began to arrive at Farmington. The priest in charge of this Mission secured for the consideration of $200.00 the following property for church purposes: This indenture made and entered into this 8th day of September A.D. 1905, by and between Sylvester R. Blake, widower, of the County of San Juan, Territory of New Mexico (New Mexico would not be a state for several more years), party of the first part, and Peter Bourgade, the present Roman Catholic Archbishop of the Diocese of Santa Fe in the United States, party of the second part. Witnessth: That the party of the first part for and in consideration of $200.00 to him in hand paid and other good and valuable considerations to him moving has and does hereby grant, bargain, sell, align, remise, release, convey, and confirm under the said party of the second part and his lawful successors in the Arch-Episcopal office in trust for the benefit of the Roman Catholic Church and said archdiocese all of the following described real estate and property situated in the County of San Juan and the territory of New Mexico, to-wit:

"Beginning 30 feet South and 30 feet West of the Southwest corner of the Town of Farmington. Thence 210 feet West parallel, etc.

"In witness thereof the party of the first part has set his hand seal, this the day and year in this instrument above written. Signed: Sylvester R. Blake."

By 1909 a new chapel was already being built by the parishioners. They received a $150.00 gift from the Extension Society and other donations of about $500 were given by various individuals.

Father Garnier writes: "I bought a bed and covers, necessary for spending a night there (in Farmington)."

For the next four or five years, the Catholic community kept building on to the chapel and even began to build a small school. By the end of December 1910, the parish was $512.00 in debt, the parish having borrowed from several people in the town. The school became the center of attention and was being built in earnest by 1913, after the Franciscans arrived to man the parish. The ledgers seem to indicate that regular collections were being taken for the building of the school. It shows that the Franciscans in Cincinnati gave $800 towards a new school building and other people gave $1.25 to $2.10 for a sum total of $903.00 toward the new school.

Father Albert Daeger with Father Fintan after 1910. Father Daeger was the first Franciscan pastor of Sacred Heart. Father Fintan built the present church, parish center and rectory.

The original white-framed chapel was also used for the school, readied by Father Garnier and the people before the Franciscans took over the parish.. On Oct. 2, 1910, the following message was read to the people of the parish at Mass: "Tomorrow is the beginning of parochial school.

All those who have children of school age should send their children. There will be no school money to pay. So there is no excuse unless it be the distance from here. For the present we shall use the chapel for the school. It will be a little inconvenient, of course, there being no desks and other sundries, but we hope that all will be remedied in time. The only outlay you will have to present is for the books. I shall try my skill at teaching, and though I have not a territorial or district diploma, I daresay I will get along. So, send your children and I will do my best to take care of them."

Father Fintan used one of the small rooms in the rear of the church in those early days as a classroom and taught the children himself. He frequently acted in the capacity of pastor, schoolteacher and cook.

The little school continued to prosper and after a few years of the Franciscan leadership and the growth of the town of Farmington, Father Fintan made arrangements with the Ursuline Sisters of Maple Mount, Kentucky, to send sisters into the San Juan Basin for the education of the youth in the small Catholic school. The "Red Apple," the train from Durango to Farmington, brought the nine travel-weary Sisters to the little town. The newcomers were not too favorably impressed. Driving away from the station, in company with Father Fintan and Gonzaga Wethington, a pioneer in Farmington who met them too, the Sisters had their first view of the town. It was a town of less than 800 people at that time. There were no paved streets and Main Street hardly seemed to merit that name. There were grocery stores, dry goods stores, drug stores and other places of business like First National Bank.

The Sisters recalled, in the book "Candles of the Lord," written by Sister Mary Michael Barrow, that there were Native Americans everywhere — "old men, young men, and children; squaws in their colorful voluminous skirts and bright hued blankets; papooses on cradle-

The old Sacred Heart Church and rectory about 1916 with Father Fintan and another unidentified priest. This church was where Drake Drilling is now located

boards. There were olive-skinned Spanish Americans too. Of course there were Anglos from about every state. Such was the cosmopolitan little Farmington of yesteryear . . ."

The Sisters were eager to see the church and the school. The small combination frame church, rectory and school "were not the imposing edifices which are a credit to Farmington now," Sister Mary Michael wrote in 1949. "On the contrary both church and school were extremely humble in their exterior appearance, as well as modestly frugal in their interior furnishings. Just about what one would expect to find in a small Western town where there were very few Catholics, all making a brave struggle to get started in life admidst pioneer surroundings.

The Sisters did not have a convent when they arrived, but rather they occupied rooms at the San Juan Community Hospital, which was easy walking distance from the church and school on Pinon Avenue.

"On the Feast of Our Lady's Dolors in early September, the hospital staff welcomed the three sisters who came to take possession of their new quarters. The other six sisters who had arrived with them were divided between Waterflow and Blanco in their work. The three sisters in Farmington were Sister Margaret Mary, who was to teach in the school; Sister Antoinette, who would join the nurses' staff; and Sister Veronica, who was to aid in the diet kitchen.

Nine students assembled for classes in September 1919 but within a short period of time, so many children were trying to get into the school that Sister Mary Michael said that "classes soon reached such proportions as to render the small school building really inadequate. Not only did the Catholics of Farmington patronize the Sisters[1] school, but many non-Catholic children came also."

By 1920 it was more than obvious that the present property on Pinon Street was too small for the needs of the growing Catholic community. Father Fintan bought some property on the north side of the town on a hill overlooking the town. So at the time the property was bought, the present location of the church was outside the city limits. La Plata Street, which is now the southern boundary of the present property, was the northern boundary of Farmington in 1920. The property Father

First Communion, 1926 with Father Fintan, Sister Margaret Mary and Sister Dorothy.

Fintan bought was a large grape arbor which had been owned by Etta Morris. There were no other buildings in the area, except a couple of homes along Orchard Street. None of the streets were paved at this time and when the church was built in 1929, the people would come straight up Allen Street and walk, ride horses or drive right into the property up to the front door of the church.

Presently, if you start at Main Street and drive north up Allen Avenue, it lines up exactly with what used to be the church's front door. Later, when the city expanded and Allen Avenue was paved, the city had to go around the church property. This accounts for the strange jog in the street.

By 1928, there were 200 adults and 75 children coming to Sacred Heart Parish from a radius of 20 miles. In the summer of 1928, with major contributions from the Cincinnati Franciscans and money from the Extension Society and the people of the parish, Father Fintan and his people started construction.

Father Fintan had dreamed of this project long before 1928, though. As far back as 1918, according to Sister Mary Michael in her book, Mother Aloysius and Sister Robertus visited Farmington and Father Fintan "had shown them the site on the hill" where he hoped, at some future time, to build a church and school. Ten years were to pass before his hopes were realized, but the finished product was worth the delay.

According to Frances and Joe Wethington, who wrote of those early days, "before any work could be done on building the church, school and rectory, the tumbleweeds, sage brush and other debris had

Sacred Heart
Church being
built in 1928

to be cleared off the grounds of the newly-purchased land at Allen Street." After this was completed, Gonza Wethington, with his team of horses and fresno (scoop), leveled the land. Then full steam ahead. It was decided that the school should be built first so that the basement part could be used for saying the Masses. Mr. Castonguey, the only Catholic carpenter in Farmington, was hired as the foreman. His daughter, Miss Anna Castonguey, was the organist and choir director down at the old church; and of course, remained so when the new church was built. As one parishioner put it, "The choir was like listening to the angels sing."

The Wethingtons write that Dan Thomas and his two boys, Alfred and Hobert, and even Margaret, one of his daughters, put on their coveralls and worked every day digging out the gravel from the glade road which ran down to what used to be Palmer Plaza.

"Dan Thomas also did the concrete work for all the buildings. Clinton Taylor, a prominent Mormon gentleman, laid the brick for the school, the rectory and the church. Many hands went into the building of these three buildings. Much of this labor was done for gratis, but the foreman, Mr. Castonguey, received the unthinkable sum of $5.00 an hour. With this goodly sum he hired Merle Miller to be his flunky for the total sum of 50 cents an hour. The average pay for the other carpenters was $1.00 an hour. Joe Wethington worked free and hauled the sand for the concrete work and remembers doing so for two summers. He finally did get a partner to help him through the machinations of Father Fintan."

Not everything on the construction job always ran perfectly. The communion railing had to be hauled up from the depot to the newly-built church by a team of horses and wagon. Just as the last section of the railing was removed from the wagon, Sister Margaret Mary started ringing the Angelus. The horses were spooked and bolted off down the hill and across what is now Sacred Heart School's playground. They continued running between Freeman's house (the house directly south of the playground bordering Allen Avenue) and a tall poplar tree which was standing there. The horses got through the opening. The wagon did not.

The horses ran crazily up and down nearly every street in the town. Some people tried to stop the horses, but they only veered away from the people. Finally, from utter exhaustion, the horses came to an abrupt halt and were led docilely back to the church.

It wasn't unusual during the months of November, December and January during the construction time that temperatures might drop to 15 degrees or more below zero. And that was all during the day. The ground would nearly be covered at least by a foot of snow and would lay on the ground most of winter. Therefore, during these months, the construction almost came to a complete halt.

When the school and church were finished, a large amount of the Gallup yellow bricks were left over, according to the Wethingtons. Father Fintan, they said, only had permission for a school and church.

"He was standing with some men staring at the bricks and said, 'Let's build a rectory with the rest of the bricks.' 'But, Father, we don't

Pablo and Felima Baca taking Sisters Dorothy, Pierre, George Marie and Ursulita on the way to Archuleta, Colorado

Dedication of St. Thomas School, Farmington 1928

have permission.' And Father Fintan answered, 'What are they going to do, make us tear it down?"

With that, according to the Wethingtons, they "took a stick and drew the outline of the rectory in the sand."

Thus the large rectory which still houses the priests was the last of the building projects in 1929.

But there is one big catch to the above story. According to the photo found in the Parish Center main hallway, the Rectory and School/Convent were built first and the Church was built last. The photo shows clearly the rectory's west side and the fully-constructed School/Convent and the open field where the Church would eventually stand.

Though the Church was finished in 1929, the solemn blessing of Sacred Heart Church took place on Wednesday, Feb. 26, 1930, at 10 a.m. Most Rev. Albert T. Daeger, O.F.M., D.D., who was the first Franciscan pastor of Sacred Heart, came from Santa Fe to bless the Church. This was ten years before the Diocese of Gallup was established, so Farmington was in the Archdiocese of Santa Fe at the time of the blessing. Very Rev. Urban Freundt, O.F.M., the provincial of the Province of St. John the Baptist Franciscans in Cincinnati, Ohio, assisted

Archbishop Daeger with Franciscans at the dedication in 1929

Archbishop Daeger.

St. Thomas School's doors soon opened. The school was so named because a benefactor from Extension Society gave a large donation only if the school would be named St. Thomas in honor of her deceased husband.

The new school offered well-equipped classrooms and also included facilities for a limited number of boarding pupils. There was an auditorium for school activities and a spacious playground.

During the intense building projects, Archbishop Daeger of Santa Fe anxiously oversaw the project from the See City. He made it very clear in one note, on May 18, 1928, that Father Fintan was to be careful that he alone made final decisions: "As we do not recognize any 'Church Committees' do not let any LAY man sign. YOU are the Church Committee."

Of course, with the building of these three major structures — the church, the school and the rectory — there were plenty of debts which Father Fintan had to worry about. In February 1929, Archbishop Daeger wrote to Father Fintan that the documents were now on their way "for your swell LOAN OF FIFTEEN THOUSAND! And all by

Archbishop Daeger with fellow priests

Various Sisters at the church dedication.

REGISTERED MAIL! Of course, the ENGRAVED and 'steel-armored' BONDS will come in a few days — which I suppose I will have to sign — each and every one of the THIRTY, and return to St. Louis."

Archbishop Daeger writes that Father Fintan is to use his own judgment as to the fire and tornado insurance the church buildings would need.

"You will surely cut it down — otherwise I do not know HOW you will pay all the insurance premiums. As to fire I do not think it too high, but TORNADO?"

The movement of the Sisters from the small convent where they had lived for over a decade at Pinon to the new convent was bittersweet. In "Candles of the Lord," Sister Mary Michael Barrow writes: " . . . the Sisters were really loath to leave the scenes of earlier years. Sometimes they had laughingly spoken of their convent as the 'cigar box.' That little 'cigar box,' though not fashioned from rich cedar wood, held for them cherished memories — memories fragrant with the aroma of riches amidst poverty, and of peace and contentment, amidst little sacrifices cheerfully made and little crosses willingly borne. Yes, these first years held for them memories of prosperity and memories of adversity. However, 'adversity is not without comforts and hopes,' and prosperity does not always mean happiness nor goodness."

The Ursulines had a spirit still spoken of fondly today by parishioners who remember the many Sisters who passed through their lives over the years. One remembered with special fondness was Sister George Marie Morgan.

After teaching for years in Kentucky schools, her health began to fail. Hoping the healthy New Mexico climate would help her, the Superiors in the order removed her from active duty and sent her to live in Farmington at the old convent.

"Candles of the Lord" relates the story of her final years: "The tiny convent in Farmington gave a wholesome welcome to the young semi-invalid,who was rather a joy than a care to her companions. Her bright, cheerful disposition and her entire resignation to God's Holy Will, were constant sources of edification, not only to her companions, but to all who knew her. Smiling always and with a never-fading serenity, her cheerfulness persisted even when there came the realization that there was small hope of recovery.

"She was a special favorite Sister to the little children of Farmington and they came often to visit with her. To them and with them, Sister George Marie was another child — simple, gentle and very approachable. There was one little boy, himself almost an invalid, whose affection for Sister was singularly strong. Often he came . . . bringing her gifts, chickens, flowers, fruits, and sweetmeats, and when

Fathers Felician and Fintan.

she died, he was inconsolable. His parents . . . relate that their little son really never overcame his grief. It was not long before (the little boy) joined his friend in heaven.

"On Dec. 21, 1925, Sister George Marie went home to God. All that day, and particularly during the period of evening recreation, she was even more than usual, cheerful and gay. She signed and addressed Christmas greeting cards to family relatives and to members of her religious community in the East. These greeting cards reached their destination after dear little Sister George Marie lay in her grave.

"Almost without any warning, Sister suffered a severe hemorrhage from the lungs and died within minutes. There was only time for the Sisters to call Father Fintan from a nearby residence. Father came and administered the Sacraments of the dying, just as Sister was breathing her last."

Her sister, Sister Rose Alice, was stationed in Blanco at the time of Sister George Marie's death and did not receive the message of her sister's death until the following morning, as there were, then, no telephone connections with Blanco. The roads leading to Blanco were, in those days, practically impassable in the winter months.

Father Fintan offered the Requiem Mass for Sister George Marie on Dec. 23, at Sacred Heart Church on Pinon and burial took place the same day in the cemetery at Waterflow.

The Sisters began a new tradition in 1929 at the first Christmas program in the new school. The night before the Christmas program, Sister Margaret Mary, Sister Dorothy (for whom the garden beside the Parish Center is named) and Clara Zumbahlen (Father Fintan's sister and housekeeper) filled paper sacks with hard candy plus an orange as an added treat. These were given at the end of the program to every child present by Santa Claus himself. Then, on the Feast of the Epiphany, Father Fintan would give each child in the school a small sack of hard candy on the Feast which is also known as "Little Christmas."

When Father Fintan left as pastor in 1932, Father Camillus Fangmann, O.F.M., served as pastor for the next two years. Following

TOP: 8th Grade graduation from St. Thomas School in 1929. John Shannon, Merle Miller, Herbert Thomas, Lila Mae James, Sister Margaret Mary, Elizabeth Wethington, Father Fintan

CENTER: The graduating class with Sister Margaret Mary and Father Camillus.

BOTTOM: Father Fintan's ball team.

Sister Dorothy, Sister Margaret Mary with Father Fintan in front of the St. Thomas School and Convent.

him as pastor was Father Roger Hengehold, O.F.M., who served as pastor from 1935 through 1941.

Father Maurice Rippeger, O.F.M., the provincial of the Province of St. John the Baptist in Cincinnati wrote to Father Roger on Aug. 26, 1935 on the Pinon old church property: "Yesterday Father Fintan spoke to me about the contemplated sale of the old church property to some Mexican for the sum of $1,500.00 You have my consent provided you also get the permission of Archbishop Gerken (of Santa Fe). You might tell his Excellency that Archbishop Daeger had already given permission. But insist that the Mexican pay the whole sum in cash. Otherwise I fear you will never get the money. With this money you would be able to pay your debt to Parkview, which must be done since Father Theodosius needs the money for the completion of his church and you would have a nice little sum left to apply on your other debts."

Father Roger spent a good part of his time as pastor striving to pay off the debts of the parish and, according to correspondence, seemed to do well in this regard. Father Edward Leary, O.F.M., served as pastor from 1942 to 1943, when Father Anthony Kroger took over the reigns from 1944 to 1946.

When Father Anthony was at Sacred Heart, an interesting turn of events took place. Suddenly the deeply admired and much loved

Father Fintan returned yet again in residence on sick leave. This happened often in these years. For instance, In 1939, Father Fintan had returned for his health and stayed two more years, left again and returned in 1944 for yet another year of sick leave. The rectory at Sacred Heart was large and the porches on both ends were used for sick Franciscans who came to the Southwest to recover from many ailments, including lung ailments. The Franciscan ledgers list Eusebius Schweitzer, O.F.M., as also being at Sacred Heart in residence on sick leave.

Having Father Fintan live in residence was a mixed blessing for Father Anthony. Though Father Fintan could help some in the parish, his prominence and strong opinons seemed to get in the pastor's way at times. Bishop Bernard Espelage, the first bishop of Gallup (Gallup became a diocese in 1939), wrote to him on August 2, 1945, about paying off the parish debt, which continued to plague those who followed Father Fintan. "Just tell (Father Adalbert—the financial secretary for the Province of St. John the Baptist) that you are trying to straighten out your books and you would like to know just how you stand. They are somewhat peeved back there (in Cincinnati) about this business, as the Province payed (sic) off the bonds on the church and school in the amount of $6,000 and asked Father Roger (Henegold) when he was pastor (1935-1941) to sign a note for this amount and he refused. This is just a little tip I am giving you."

Then Bishop Espelage gets to the matter of Father Fintan: "I am sure that you are glad of the transfer of Father Fintan. This move will be good for the parish as well as for you. I presume that there are some who do not like it, but that will pass over. I got a long letter from L.L. Stallings about the change. I answered that I had nothing to do with the change and these changes are made by the Provincial. It is good that Clara is leaving too. (Clara was Father Fintan's sister and had been housekeeper at Sacred Heart for years.) . . Try to take care of yourself and don't worry about what is being said about Fintan's change. It will die out."

By August 18, 1945, Father Anthony has obviously become more concerned with bad feelings left at the leaving of the famous Father

Fintan. Bishop Espelage wrote to him on this date: "As to the present tense feeling I would just ignore them alltogether (sic) and act in everything as if nothing happened. I would never refer to the transfer in any way either in public or in private. That fact that Clara (Father Fintan's sister) is staying there may make matters worse, but I would even ignore this too. I would do the same with regard to the Sisters."

It was not always easy for the pastor to deal with the Religious Sisters either, it seems. In a letter which seems to have been written by Father Theodosius Meyer, he speaks of "some of the padres" being "not quite open and above-board, some of the Sisters are old fixtures . . ."

This priest, who served one year as pastor from 1947 to 1948 (though his term must have spilled a bit into the year 1949, because there are two letters from him in that time) does not seem to be having a good day. He states in the February 1949 letter that the "Farmington climate and I are not getting along so well. I have been going on borrowed time the last two weeks — dangerously near pneumonia, nervous and on edge. Besides 'people are funny' and many of the people here in the San Juan Valley are very funny. Maybe it would be better expressed, they are 'difficult.' A little on the ignorant side, they are selfish, full of distrust and suspicion, some of them are smart-alecks and buttinskis."

Father Theodosius states that the children are "self-willed (to say it nicely). The old folks are set in their ways, and I am a little too old to be a trouble-shooter, to take hold of a run-down place, full of dissension, make it over into a smooth-running organization, and then be sent into another difficult place."

Father Fintan's Silver Jubilee, Sacred Heart, Farmington

A view of the city ball field in the 1940s with the church, rectory (middle roof) and parish center.

Father Theodosius seems deeply troubled about the continued debts of the parish. "It makes it bad for me, because the people had been led to believe that there was no debt remaining. I argued it out with them last year. . .This business of saying that maybe it was written off so as not 'to place an intolerable burden on the priest in charge' at that time does not set so well with me. Why take the burden off others and then saddle it on to me, thus imposing on good nature?"

Father Theodosius, who was born in Batesville, Indiana in 1882 and was ordained a priest in 1914, worked in the Southwest missions throughout his life: Santa Fe, Roswell, Lumberton, Parkview, Pena Blanca, Farmington, Cuba and Gallup. He also had charge of several outlying missions: Hagerman, Elida, Portales, Clovis and Melrose. Father Theodosius seemed to recover his health after leaving Farmington and continued on for another decade and from 1951 to 1953 served as chaplain of the Poor Clares in Roswell. He died on April 1, 1958.

Following Father Theodosius Meyer was a true character of a priest, Father Theophil Meyer, O.F.M., who came to Sacred Heart in 1949 and then remained until 1957. Stories are still told of this man who preached like a lion from the pulpit, pounding the podium for dramatic effect. Some swear he could be heard all the way down on

The wedding of Mary Lou Keenan to Fred Edwards, August 13, 1949. Celebrant was Father Theodosius Meyer. Servers were Bill Schnorr and Tim Foster. Seated in pew on left is Sister Margaret Mary.

Main Street when the windows were open in the church on hot summer days. He was deeply loved by the children of the parish. They swarmed all around him on the playground whenever he made a visit.

He is the center of many stories around Farmington. People tell of him admonishing them to sit down when they tried to leave early from Mass or if they were a moment or so late for Mass, addressing them directly to be seated or stopping in the middle of the homily and waiting for them to shrink embarrassed into the nearest pew.

But there are stories of him also being so kind to the "least among us" and having a great heart for little children. He was on the portly side and Father Vincent, writing a letter from the Office of the Treasurer for the Franciscan Fathers in Cincinnati, Ohio, ribs him at the end of the letter dated November 12, 1949: "Keep your faith and your courage up, your weight down, and your feet on the ground."

It was Father Theophil who in the Spring of 1956 had informal talks with Bishop Espelage about building the present Sacred Heart School. Bishop Espelage was reluctant for the parish to go into debt, obviously knowing the burdens shouldered by many priests after the building of the original three large structures by Father Fintan. So the Men's Club of the parish had the idea of having a pledge drive to get the money together before the school would be built.

In the summer of 1956 the Men's Club started the drive to see how much money they could get together for the new school. At first they thought they would not build any more than they could pay for. But the needs of the growing community and school made them decide that they had to go out on a limb and build what was needed. In the Fall of 1956, the Building and Planning Committee (Oscar Thomas, I.J. Coury, Dr. Reilly, Angelo Turano, Frank Sattler and Frank Deiterman) met with the bishop.

Bishop Espelage made it clear that if the pledge drive was not successful that the construction of the school would stop. Besides the pledge drive, a series of bingo parties were held in the basement of St. Thomas School.

By the end of the pledge drive, the people had pledged approximately $40,000 for the building fund for the new school. During the winter months of 1957, plans were made and approved for the building and a bid was received from Hesselden Construction Company for $135,000.

Bishop Espelage, though obviously nervous about the parish going into deep debt, gave the go-ahead for construction with $48,000 in the building fund, a $30,000 loan, $10,000 in a savings account and $7,000 in a general account.

The church, therefore, had about $95,000 of the $135,000 needed for construction and Bishop Espelage would not sign the loan from the bank for the rest of the money. The Men's Club didn't let this get them down. Instead they met and came up with an idea: The money would be borrowed in the name of the parish, but in case of default, each of the men would sign the note and be responsible for up to $2,000 each.

Construction began in earnest then. By August 12, 1957, Father Kenneth Robertson, drove up to Farmington from his last assignment in Laguna to take over from Father Theophil as the new pastor of Sacred

Heart Church. He would pastor Sacred Heart until 1963, during a large growth spurt in Farmington. In 1950 there had been a mere 3,000 people. Due to the oil and gas boom of the 1950s, though, the town by 1956 had grown to 20,000 people.

In the Fall of 1957, the old St. Thomas School served the students until the new school was completely finished. The major part of the construction was done by November. Important finishing touches were still

Father Kenneth Robertson

needed and the Men's Club struggled to help with these items.

In January 1958, some of the classes were able to move into the still unfinished school. During the summer of 1958, Venetian blinds were installed and the floor of the gym was painted.

On Sept. 2, 1958, all classes moved to the new school and on Sunday, Sept. 7, 1958, the school was formally dedicated by Bishop Espelage. On Feb. 1, 1960, the note was paid off for the new school. The large debt was paid off in three years due to the hard work, sacrifice and dedication of the parishioners.

By February 1960, permission was granted to add four more classrooms to the lower level of the school because of the sudden growth in student enrollment. By August 28, 1961, there were 510 children in the school from grades 1 to 8.

By 1961, Farmington had grown by leaps and bounds and talk began that Sacred Heart Church was simply too small to take care of the Catholic population of the city. There were over 1,100 people attending

Mass each Sunday at Sacred Heart in the little church which only seated 200 people.

At this time there were seven Masses on Sunday to accomodate the mass of people. Finally Bishop Espelage gave permission to build another church in town to relieve the problem.

In the Parish Bulletin of Nov. 15, 1961, Father Kenneth wrote: "After several months of prayer and deliberations the contract for the new church was signed this past Wednesday, October the 11th, 1961, in a negotiated contract with the contractor, Kealy Construction. Ceremonial ground-breaking will be announced in the near future. The maximum cost of the new church is $190,000.00 Please pray daily for the complete success of your new church in which God will always be honored and adored by you."

Ten acres of ground were purchased from El Paso Gas Company on 20th Street for $30,000. In the Spring of 1962, the construction on St. Mary's Church began. By the Fall of 1962, the church was near completion. Early on the morning of Dec. 8, 1962, Father Kenneth privately blessed the new St. Mary's Church prior to the first Mass to be held there that day.

The first Mass was at 9:30 a.m., followed by Masses at 11 a.m. and 7 p.m.

The official dedication of the church would be in the Spring of 1963. At first there were no weekday Masses in the church on 20th Street. The weekday Masses were all held at Sacred Heart.

The priests of Sacred Heart celebrated Masses for both churches in those early days. On March 10, 1963, there was the solemn dedication of St. Mary's Church by Bishop Espelage with a dinner following in Sacred Heart School Gym.

1963 was a big year for one of the most famous of the Ursuline Sisters in Farmington. The parish bulletin reported this on April 14, 1963: "Sister Dorothy celebrates her Golden Jubilee tomorrow. 50 years in Religious Life! 50 years as an Ursuline Sister! Forty of these years have been spent in Farmington. The whole parish joins in heartfelt congratulations for Sister Dorothy today."

Father Gerard Geier, O.F.M., served for one year after Father Kenneth was transferred in 1963. In 1964 Father Ronnin Einhaus became pastor until Father Kenneth returned as pastor in 1972. Father Kenneth remained as pastor until 1981.

On May 25, 1976, it was announced by Father Kenneth that St. Mary's had become its own parish, no longer under the careful watch of the Mother Church of Sacred Heart. Effective June 1, 1976, Father Kenneth wrote in the bulletin in May, "Butler Avenue will be the dividing line, thus the area West of Butler Avenue will officially be Sacred Heart Parish, while the area East of Butler Avenue will officially be St. Mary's Parish."

In late May, Monsignor James Lindenmeyer arrived as the first pastor of the new parish. For the present time, the rectory and parish office was at 2212 East 12th Street.

On June 1, 1976, Bishop Jerome Hastrich, who was the second bishop of Gallup, officially divided the parishes.

In 1977, Father Kenneth could focus his attention on Sacred Heart, now that St. Mary's had its own pastor. He spoke at all the Masses on May 15, 1977, advising the parishioners of the projected addition to the church building to seat an additional 200 people.

Permision was granted by the Provincial Definitorium and Bishop Hastrich in June 1977 to remodel the church for the accomodation of more people. By October 19, 1977, the whole rear wall of the church building was pulled down. By January 1978, the new portion of the church was joined up with the old, with the dismantling of the old sanctuary floor and ceiling. Pews were moved into the gym.

By March 17, 1978, the bricklayers had completed the brick facing on the new addition to the church. The carpenters were still working on the outside of the addition. Carpeting in the nave and the sanctuary of the church was completed. On April 3, 1978, a truckload of 46 pews for the church arrived from Waco, Texas.

On April 14, 1978, everything for the Mass was transferred to the church and on April 15, the first Mass in the renovated church would be held at 8:15 a.m. The old pews were sent to the Indian Chapel in Albuquerque.

On Sunday, April 16, 1978, the church was blessed and rededicated at 5:30 p.m. with Bishop Jerome J. Hastrich officiating and with the four living ex-pastors as the concelebrants: Father Kenneth Robertson, Father Theophil Meyer, Father Gerard Geier and Father Ronnin Einhaus.

Father Kenneth was able to lengthen the church without changing dramatically any part of it. The sanctuary was simply duplicated. One can only tell that a renovation took place by the seam which crosses the large vaulted ceiling.

After 16 years in the parish as pastor, in 1981 the Franciscans transferred the beloved Father Kenneth. Father Dacian Batt replaced him as shepherd of the parish.

"One of the first impressions I had as I drove in the main entrance at Apache and Allen and drove around the rectory and to the Parish Center and toward the church was that this was an asphalt jungle," he said. "Everything was blacktopped right up to the Parish Center to all the walls of the church up to the high cement wall looking into Sister Dorothy's garden. It seemed strange that out here in the Land of Enchantment that everything would be blacktopped like in the middle of the inner city."

Father Dacian spent a large part of his pastorate, therefore, landscaping the areas nearest the church to break up this "inner city" look.

It was also during his time as pastor that the Sisters of St. Agnes were brought to work at Sacred Heart Parish. In August 1986 Sisters Mariana Frigo and Lael Niblick were assigned to the parish as coordinators of religious education. Sister Marianna was responsible for the pre-school and elementary levels while Sister Lael was responsible for the junior and senior high levels. Sister Lael also served as youth minister. In 1986 the number of children in the program was around 200.

Sister Lael arrived with her parents in a rented trailer. The house which the parish had purchased for the Sisters was at 401 North Orchard Avenue.

In August 1987, Sister Marianna was transferred to Wisconsin and Sister Rene Backe replaced her as coordinator of CCD with Sister Lael. The Sisters then moved out of the little house and into a larger one on the corner of Apache and Orchard Streets. The religious education program grew and, as Sister Rene relates, there was "a yearly blessing disguised as a problem . . . finding enough room for all the children and youth who participated. That blessing is still with us today."

The youth programs grew in numbers. Sacred Heart youth participated in many diocesan youth programs. Sister Lael brought NET (National Evangelization Team) to Farmington to give a youth retreat.

Sister Lael liked to explore and the attic of the Parish Center held treasures. She held a rummage sale and then cleaned up the attic. The bell that used to hang in the tower of the parish center now hangs in the Catholic school in Waspam, Nicaragua.

In all of these projects, the people of Sacred Heart were very supportive, Sister Rene said.

Sister Lael began giving guitar lessons so the children could play for the school Masses. She also developed a love for and a skill in sailing with Father Dacian in his boat. Sister Rene did not possess the

Father Dacian Batt and Father Paul Juniet, Franciscans, with parishioners, in the early 1990s

Altar servers from the early 1990s

same skill, and one afternoon she recalled that while sailing with Father Dacian, a storm came up.

"The thunder, lightning, rain, hail could not get Father Dacian to return to land," she remembered. "Finally the wind capsized the boat and both Father Dacian and I went into the lake. After clinging to the boat for what seemed like half a day, we finally got to shallow enough water to stand and upright the boat. It was several years before I went sailing with Father Dacian again."

Father Dacian asked Sister Rene to research various kinds of parish renewal programs and in 1990, Sacred Heart Parish began the national program known as RENEW. A core team was formed and many parishioners participated in the small group Scripture sharing sessions which were the heart of the program.

"There was a real hunger for the Word of God in many parishioners at that time," Sister Rene said. "Also, in the late '80s and through the '90s, Sacred Heart sponsored and Sister Rene organized annual weekend retreats.

Father Dacian served as pastor until 1992 when Father Meldon Hickey was named the transitional pastor until the Diocese of Gallup would have its diocesan priests take over the parish. Over a decade before the Franciscans left Sacred Heart Parish, the Franciscans had asked that the Diocese of Gallup take possession of the parish for the first time since 1910. The Franciscans wanted to center their work in the missionary parishes, not in the larger towns and cities which they knew were self-sufficient. Bishop Donald Pelotte, the third Bishop of Gallup, asked that the Franciscans stay until he could consult on how this new parish for diocesan priests would be handled. He did not wish to rush a diocesan priest into the parish overnight and the Franciscans agreed.

Father Meldon Hickey

On September 1, 1995, eighty-five years after the Franciscans had taken possession of the parish from Father Garnier and the Archdiocese of Santa Fe in 1910, the Franciscans now handed the parish back into diocesan hands.

Before their departure, on Aug. 20, 1995, Fathers Meldon Hickey, Paul Juniet and Richard Baumann, the last three Franciscans to man the parish, joined with Bishop Donald Pelotte and Franciscan and diocesan priests from the Diocese of Gallup and beyond to remember the good work of the padres over 85 years.

Father Paul Juniet, who had served six years at Sacred Heart, stated that the farewell Mass and the reception at the Civic Center for 600 people afterwards "was nice and it was a way, as we were leaving, to celebrate the gift we were."

On Sept. 1, 1995, Father Tim Farrell became the first diocesan pastor in 85 years. His assistant pastor was Father Joe Blonski. In two years, Father Blonski was transferred and soon afterwards, Father Raymond Mahlmann arrived at Sacred Heart to live in residence and serve as chaplain to the hospital and other medical facilities.

It was a scarey thing for Father Farrell to take over the parish, he remembers. "How do you follow such a class act? Eighty-five years of Franciscan priests working in the parish, loved deeply by the people, hard workers in the vineyard of the Lord. I prayed to God that I simply do my best and hopefully that was enough. It was not easy. But, with God's help and the good people of this parish, we survived a difficult, emotionally-wrenching transition. I remember a person coming up to me my first day and asking, 'So, Father, what is your five-year plan?' I was dumbfounded. I simply said, 'I have no five-year plan. I guess I will wake up tomorrow, celebrate Mass, and do what I can do tomorrow for the Lord. I don't even have a one-day plan.' I don't think I impressed that person very much. But I believe that I am only an instrument. I wake up and do the Lord's work one day at a time. He does the rest."

Father Farrell said that he believed that he simply had to build on the past in shepherding his people. "Sacred Heart Parish has such a long and profound history. I think it was my duty to carry that tradition and history along. When things needed to be done, the Lord would make it pretty evident in His own time. I believe in building on all the good works which have been done before we came on the scene."

Soon after Father Farrell arrived, though, he was being asked by members of the parish what could be done to alleviate the overcrowding at the Masses.

"Not only did we have a problem with overcrowding at the Masses, but we really had no adequate spaces to meet. The Parish Center, the old St. Thomas School, was overused over many years. We didn't even have a stove to cook food for fundraisers if need be. We were a parish of about 3,000 people and we had a church which could hold at most 350 people at a Mass. We had no place to have luncheons for funerals. We had no place to hold wedding receptions. We had between 450 and 500 young people in CCD each Wednesday and we

The church prior to the renovation in 2001

were using any space we could find to teach those students. It seemed the Lord was trying to tell us to accomodate these people."

Soon after Father Farrell arrived, in consultation with the Parish Pastoral Council, a Building Committee was formed. This committee was charged with simply looking at the needs of the parish and reporting back to the Council.

"The problem we had was we were boxed in on this property," he explained. "Eventually, that problem was solved when we were able to buy the Dustin property on Orchard Street. Then we had a large property with which to work. After that, the architects could be hired to do a master plan for the entire property."

The Parish Council and Finance Board of the parish, along with the Building Committee, in 2000 agreed to hire Rick Bennett of Albuquerque and Tim Christensen of Farmington to work as a team in drawing up a master plan.

Though originally the Parish Council wished the Parish Center be built first, it eventually was decided that with money available, the

The western wall with overhang of the parish center before renovation.

Church had to be renovated first. A fundraising drive was to be held to strive to collect $1.4 million to build the new family center complex and renovate the old St. Thomas School as a part of the parish center complex.

On April 15, 2001, the final Mass in the church was held prior to Jaynes Corporation, the contractor for the project, fencing off the site and the people moving to the School Gymnasium for approximately six months of Sunday Masses. Daily Masses were held in the old St. Thomas School in the Franciscan Room in the basement of the building.

"I remember well that day, April 15, 2001," Father Farrell said. "Though there was an excitement about the renovation taking place, there was a profound sadness or uncertainty in me and in the people who walked through the church after Mass that day. It was Easter Sunday and though it was the Resurrection of the Lord, I guess we all felt in a way like we were still in the tomb. I remember people taking pictures of the church, quietly walking through the church, their old friend, upstairs and downstairs, all afternoon. I left the church open all day so people could come by and say farewell to the church for the months we would be in the Gymnasium. And they certainly came that day."

On Monday, April 16, all the statues and other sacred items of the church were placed in the basement of the rectory. The Tabernacle

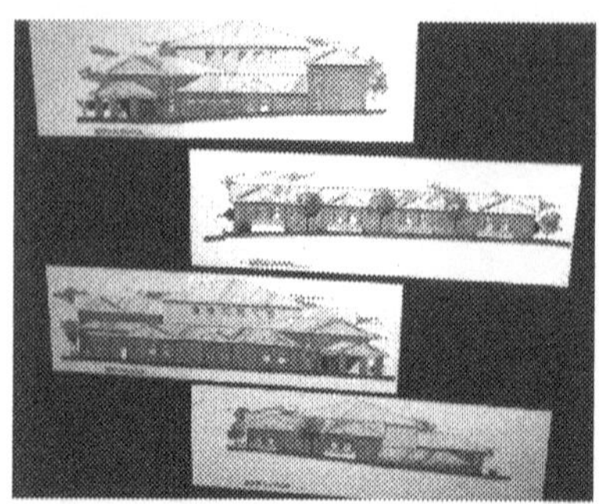

The architectural drawings of the Family Center by Rick Bennet, the architect wtih Tim Christensen on the renovation project.

and the Blessed Sacrament were placed in the Religious Education Center in a tiny chapel set up by the staff.

"Every Saturday evening, Father Ray Mahlmann would with great dignity and solemnity carry the tabernacle over to the Gymasium and set it on a little table we had there. Kris Chavez would come in the afternoon or evening on Saturdays to set up 400 chairs in the Gym for the Sunday Masses. Then after the 6 p.m. Mass we would ask the people at that Mass to help us take the chairs down and they would enthusiastically help out and the chairs would be stacked neatly and quickly in their proper places. Then the Tabernacle would be taken back up to the Religious Education Center until the next Saturday afternoon."

Confessions during this time were held in the Franciscan Room.

"With all the construction going on, it was very difficult for people to find us in our makeshift confessional. But somehow they did. At first I would tape signs around to tell the people, but the New Mexico winds would always blow them away. And, even with no signs to show the way, the people found the makeshift confessional. It amazed me, too, that I never heard a complaint during those months. People came to the Gymnasium and worshipped as they always had. They were real troopers."

A senior in high school at the time of the renovation and temporary move to the gymnasium, Neil Antonson remembers worshipping in the Gym: "(The Gym) took some time to get accustomed to, but the Masses still proved to be just as eloquent and as spiritually rewarding as before. The cold, damp and concrete floors took some time to grow on us, but now the Gym will be sorrowfully missed and will always have a place in our memory."

Daily Masses were held in the Parish Center Franciscan Room during the church renovation in 2001

Father Mahlmann remembers well the renovation project: "The experience of Sunday Masses in the Gymasium was formative for our parish family. It implied some hardships which we overcame to celebrate the Eucharist. We were made stronger for the experience."

During the renovation, Father Farrell and Father Mahlmann were given hard hats to wear so that during weekly meetings they could visit the renovation site to answer questions or voice concerns.

"I got so used to wearing that hard hat that I would forget I'd have it on and would be walking around the property, even in my house with it on," Father Farrell remembers. "Someone would say to me, 'Nice hat, Father!' and I'd find out I'd been wearing that thing and then I'd snatch it off. Before Jaynes gave me my own hard hat, a little boy at Sacred Heart School gave me a white hard hat and he had pasted the dove on it. I keep that in my collection of important things in my life."

Mary Johnson, who had much to do with the interior design and color scheme of the renovated church, said that the project of renovation was "an exciting and wonderful time for all of us at Sacred Heart. I have been very happy to be involved in this vibrant and growing parish. . . The architects did a superior job of enlarging our space while maintaining and enhancing the homey feeling Sacred Heart is known for. The construction team did an outstanding job of shaping all the plans into reality. Each of us at Sacred Heart has had a part in this project, whether it was prayer, support, monetary contributions, ideas and

Father Tim Farrell with parishioners after Sunday Mass during the church renovation. Sunday Masses were held in the school gym for six months in 2001

suggestions, working on one of the committees, or working directly on the construction itself. . . We worked as a family to make a dream come true for the honor and glory of our awesome God."

Timothy Christensen, one of the architects and a member of the LDS Church, was the architect at the weekly construction meetings and was also the on-site architect all during the project, sometimes visiting the site three or four times a week.

He said that what he noticed about the Sacred Heart project was that "it is one of the very few instances in my profession where people pray for the success of the project. I can testify that this project has benefited from the prayers offered during design and construction of this building. I told my wife that on this project even when things go wrong they always seem to turn out right. Time and time again, problems that seemed too big to solve were solved and the work went forward."

Christensen said that he gave a lot of credit to the teamwork he had with Jaynes Corporation and more especially Daniel Sedillo, who was Jaynes' man-on-the-job.

"Daniel Sedillo has been in the trenches of this project from the beginning to the end and deserves much of the credit for its successful completion. Because of the nature of this project — a remodeling of an old building with many unknowns and hidden problems — there have been many little and big problems that have cropped up during construction and many changes that have had to be made as the work progressed. Daniel treated this church as his baby from the beginning and has worked very hard to make things come out right."

Christensen said that as a child growing up on North Allen Street, he saw a lot "of this old church. My friend, Billy Putnam, was Catholic and a member of this Parish. I remember waiting for Billy outside the church while he attended Mass and wondering what went on in there. Every time I walked to the movies, I walked by this church. To me, the church is part of the background of my memories of growing up in Farmington. It is rare to be able to work on a building project that involves changing a part of personal history."

Christensen said that the building project was "an outgrowing of the faithfulness and goodness of the members of Sacred Heart Parish. As the project progressed and some of the detail of the work revealed the work of previous projects and long-gone craftsmen, I began to see the church not only in terms of its present members but as a part of the historical setting that formed the background of my youth. This church not only represents the good work of its present members, but also a great heritage of generations of good and faithful Sacred Heart Parishioners."

Rick Bennett, the other architect on the project, explained his vision this way: "Architectural design in the truest sense is a combination of effort and people. The architect often envisions what the space can be and seeks direction to establish the parameters of what a good design should be for this project. I think we were blessed with having a group of people with a common goal. The goal was to preserve the intimacy and integrity of the historic church and yet accommodate twice the congregation seating."

He said that in the design process, architectural elements "should only be used to enhance that feel. The domed ceiling, the pitched roof, the repetitive gables, the symmetrical expansion of the

The side walls of the church were removed early on in the late Spring of 2001 in order to build eastward and westward to add seating room in the church.

building in both directions with the focal point to the altar are elements that were used to save the integrity and bring this church into the 21st Century." He said he felt fortunate to work with Tim Christensen.

"We were also fortunate enough to work with the membership of the building committee to receive constant input, support and constructive criticism. Finally, we were fortunate enough to work with Father Tim. This is the second renovation that we've worked on together (Bennett also was architect on Father Farrell's parish church in St. Johns, Arizona in 1993-94). The success comes from having a pastor who understands the makeup of the parish to the point where it can be reflected in the physical building by knowing what this church means to the people and what the church can continue to mean for future generations. I feel this church is a part of us. Whenever you design something and you put the effort into it that you really should, it becomes a part of your family. As an extension of that, I have become a part of this parish family. I'll always come to Farmington and no matter what my task is, always drive by the church."

Roy Waters, who was president of the Parish Pastoral Council and on the Building Committee at the time of the church renovation, said it was a privilege "both as a parishioner and an engineer to be involved with the church remodel. . . We have a wonderful family parish

The interior of the church in the summer of 2001 during the renovation

and I think our family atmosphere and the integrity of the church has been preserved."

Brian Cornford, project manager for Jaynes Corporation said that the project was a great success due to the teamwork: "There has been a great team effort throughout the project between the architects Tim Christensen and Rick Bennett, Father Tim (Farrell), Robert Childers, Daniel (Sedillo) and myself with Jaynes, as many decisions were made regarding different aspects of the project. We held weekly planning meetings at the project where problems were solved and issues were discussed that involved this same group of people, as well as the subcontractors when the meetings involved them. These meetings always began with a prayer. This was especially enjoyable for me as I always felt that the spirit of the Lord was with us throughout the project." He said he remembers distinctly the demolition of east and west walls of the building for the expansion.

"Daniel (Sedillo) and I discussed several different ideas and methods of how to remove the exterior walls of the old existing building and in turn support the existing roof. I recall crawling around in the attic, Daniel and I, before the bid to see how the existing structure was constructed and brainstorming how to support the roof. Daniel and I both were a little skeptical and somewhat fearful at times wondering if the ideas we thought of would work. I am sure many of you saw the church at the beginning stages when it looked just like a roof standing there without walls. Well, to make a long story short, the ideas worked and this church is standing bigger and better."

Daniel Sedillo said of the project: "I have been a carpenter for over 30 years, a carpenter's son and a carpenter's grandson. I can tell you that in my heart there is no greater, more special or more noble a labor than to do what we have done here, to build the house of the Lord."

He said that for him the project was not just a job but a "special mission." "We answered to a special Boss. I am pleased to say today, we have served the Lord and all of you well, with the early, successful completion of this beautiful project." Sedillo said that there sometimes exists "a pre-conceived notion of how a typical construction worker acts and many of us have fostered that negative reputation by our behavior. However, on this project we were a kinder, gentler flock guided by a higher purpose and a labor of love. We had no serious injuries thanks to your many prayers. I was afraid there for a while that we may never complete this poject because of the constant stream of food sent over in appreciation from Father Tim in the form of donuts, burritos, pizza and fried chicken. We're not used to this and I feared that my workers may never want to leave this project."

He said that he didn't think there would ever be another project "in my career as special in my heart as this one has been. This one is for you Mom. I know you are pleased. And for you Dad. I know you are watching."

Robert Childers, a building contractor himself, served on the Building Committee. He was the parish's Building Committee representative and met weekly with the construction team. He said he was pleased with the outcome of the project. "Its hard to express how much an honor it was for me to serve, and to work with the many different people involved with the renovation and expansion of Sacred Heart. In this fast-paced world we live in, sometimes it's hard to find the time to do all the different things we would like to do, but I found myself looking

James Joe, an artist from Shiprock, New Mexico, is shown with his mother and nephew working on the Trinity paintings which are now in the vestibule of the church.

forward to the weekly meetings. . . The time needed always seemed to be there. Anytime we make a change in our lives we always wonder if it will turn out for the best. I wondered if Sacred Heart would still feel like the church I received my sacraments in and if the altar would have the same look and feeling as it did when I was married and my children received their sacraments. I prayed that my children could continue to experience the same closeness that is felt in the parish now. But because home is where the heart is, and so many peoples' hearts fill this church, I felt it would always be home. . . I think the church turned out better than any of us could have hoped for."

Father Farrell remembers near-disaster striking near the end of the construction project.

"It was one of those odd evenings. It was dusk and Father Ray had to get to the hospital and I had to go somewhere. Anyway, my dog Rainy needed a walk and Father Ray and I had to discuss some parish business. So we all three walked over to the little park across Allen Avenue from the Church and we talked maybe ten minutes. Coming around the back of the church, I suddenly got this oddest of feelings, like something was very wrong. Turning the corner, I saw the dumpster on fire and the flames were shooting higher than the roof. Father Ray called 911 and the Fire Department was there almost immediately. If Father Ray had gone to the hospital, if I had headed immediately to where I was supposed to be going, I think very likely the almost finished church would have gone up in flames. Hot pieces of garbage were swirling around and flying through the windows of the church. Inside the church, the workers had been painting and refinishing the doors. There were pasted signs all over the place, 'Fire Danger.' The fire crew walked through the darkened church with me and we found no problems. It was miraculous, absolutely amazing that nothing major caught fire. I mean, the dumpster was right by the church. It seems the sun hit a rag or paper just right and started the fire. We'll never know, but the important thing is that our church and the other structures were saved. And I know the Good Lord was responsible. The old saying, 'There are no coincidences with God' proved true once again."

On Friday, Oct. 12, earlier than had been projected, the parish moved all its precious sacred items back into the church from the rectory basement where they had been placed for protection.

The night before, though, Father Farrell moved one item himself. "I love the beautiful crucifix in our church and I was able to, with Father Ray's help, hang it back up first. I will always remember how very special that was for me. Then we moved some of the statues back to where they belonged."

On "moving day" people from the parish, all during the day, moved items back into the church and cleaned the entire renovated structure.

"It was an amazing and moving thing to see, all these good people quietly and with great reverence moving everything back into the church," Father Farrell said. "I remember the moving of the tabernacle back into the church. That was when I knew we were truly home again. But all day that Friday children and adults came and helped in any way they could. There were no complaints, no vying for position. They all

The new gables are shown being completed on the west side of the church in Summer, 2001.

worked quietly in their own way to move back home. I remember the men hanging the Stations of the Cross up so lovingly. I remember the children wiping down the pews. I remember all these good works for the Lord."

The first Mass back in the renovated church was on Saturday, Oct. 13, and hundreds came to the 8:15 Mass that day. The first Sunday Mass was at 8 a.m. on Sunday, Oct. 14, 2001.

"That Sunday, we had our altar server practice. We had been in the Gym so long that we had to get use to our new surroundings in the church. The kids were great and very patient."

On Wednesday, October 24, the parish held an open house and many of those who were involved in the planning and renovating of the church attended. The evening began with an emotional slide show of the entire project put together by Michael Darmody. Then several people spoke on their feelings about the project. Father Meldon Hickey, the last Franciscan pastor at Sacred Heart, said that the renovated church was "beautiful and new and yet it is still Old Sacred Heart Church that all of us have come to know and love. I thank all of you for blending the old and the new. I know it was difficult for some of you to see even one iota of Old Sacred Heart change. But being the practical and far-sighted people you are, you realized the necessity of expanding your warm and close church."

Sister Rene Backe used the prophet Isaiah's words to speak of the renovation:

"'Enlarge the spaces of your tent. Extend the curtains of your home, do not hold back! Lengthen your ropes, make your tent-pegs firm, for you will burst out to right and left.' . . . It has been so interesting to see daiily the widening of this tent. Before the right and left could be widened, the old right and left had to go. That was the sad part, letting go, hoping and praying that the temporary beams would hold the roof up. Then the building of the new right and the new left, one brick at a time. The roof was covered one layer at a time. And did you notice that the inner layer had the word 'Grace' on every piece of it? How appropriate? Grace. Graciousness has been the inner spirit of this church, revealed externally in the welcoming spirit."

Kami Haskill, a high school student, said that "even though our church has expanded now, its not so much the building as it is the core of this church, our people. We have a living and giving parish, one I am glad to be a part of. . ."

Irene Newitt thanked all the priests and sisters who helped her over her life. "My spirituality of life is simple and natural. My Navajo way of prayer is to say Diiji aadoo taa akwiiji Hosgo Diyin kego naa sha do. 'I walk in beauty with my Lord—today and every day the best I know how.'"

Julie Madrid, a college student, said that she "will never forget the internal peace that I feel when I come to church empty or full."

On Thursday, Oct. 25th, Bishop Donald Pelotte rededicated Sacred Heart Church and blessed the altar. Father Farrell remembers that evening well.

"I had asked the bishop if 5:30 p.m. would work since it would be getting dark at that time. He said it would be fine. Well, by the time his homily was over, it was very dark. I have been told by people that it was quite dramatic. The lights in the church are not to be turned on till after the bishop's blessing of the walls and the sun, going down, shone in one brilliant beam onto the altar before dying out completely. I remember that during the blessing at Mass, the bishop was having trouble seeing, and finally a choir member, who had a tiny light, gave it to Deacon Tim Lujan, the emcee for the bishop, and then the bishop could finish. Suddenly Daniel Sedillo turned on the lights at the proper time and the church was washed with that beautiful light and I heard gasps from the people attending. We had priests and sisters and brothers and lay people from all over celebrating with us that night and they all were just overwhelmed by the beauty of our church. I still am to this day."

There was a large dinner held at the Elks Lodge and hundreds attended, Father Farrell said.

"Though it was a beautiful event, the next day I was so glad for peace and quiet. My brother Mike and his son David had come from Oklahoma to represent the family. All my family had planned to come out for the rededication, but then Sept. 11th happened the month before, the terrible events at the World Trade Center and the Pentagon, and we decided not to have any of the family fly in. Mike and David drove from Apache, Oklahoma, for the event. So on that Friday after the event, I went up to Durango with them and we had a nice, quiet day."

Bishop Pelotte, Father Farrell said, was amazed by the renovation of the church. "I remember taking him over to the church when he arrived a couple of hours before the rededication and he looked stunned, even overwhelmed. He said something like, 'This is unbelievable. It is beautiful.' Then he spent some time quietly walking all through the church, looking very carefully at each thing."

Soon after the rededication, it was decided by the Parish Pastoral Council and the Finance Board to have the Building Committee move forward on the Parish Center complex.

On August 8, 2002, the Building Committee, in consultation with Father Farrell, decided to sign a contract for $1.687 million to build a new parish center social hall with classrooms and renovate the Old St. Thomas School as a part of the whole complex.

"That was truly an experience which took my breath away. We had about $1 million in the Morgan Stanley Dean Witter account raised by the good people of the parish. And now I was putting my signature to a contract which wouldbe signed before we had the rest of the almost $700,000 needed. But Roy Waters and Cuff Sellmeyer reminded me of what we had already accomplished and that we would meet our financial needs. It would work. Have faith, they reminded me. So I signed the contract on August 8, 2002, and our fate was sealed."

Tim Christensen, Rick Bennett and Jaynes Corporation, with Daniel Sedillo overseeing this project, reteamed. The weekly building meetings were held once again. It was decided to build the new complex first and then renovate the Old St. Thomas School. Because construction did not start until September, it was imperative that the Old St. Thomas School, which had been all cleaned out for renovation first, be reentered so that CCD classes could
be held.

"Oh, I will never forget that day we cleaned out the Old Parish Center," Father Farrell said. "It was late June and hot and dry. So many teens came by to volunteer to clean and move things into the rectory basement. I remember several of the tall, young men carrying very heavy items down the stairs. I mean, if we had had to pay for this kind of help, we I d be bankrupt. But they never complained and worked so hard all day. And then the young women came and did so much cleaning and moving of items. And then there were many adults who dropped in as they could to help out. But our teens were wonderful that day. Not a complaint, not one complaint. Just hard work. Then we had pizza and cokes and by early afternoon we were done." So, though all the tables and chairs had been moved with all other items from the Old St. Thomas School to the rectory basement, in late August, many of the young men returned to move tables and chairs back to the parish center to get ready for CCD classes.

"I remember that the Mascarenas boys (Aaron and Brian) had served Mass on Sunday, Aug. 31, at the 10 a.m. Mass. Then they had brought all their buddies and cousins out after Mass to move all that stuff, chairs and tables, back over to the parish center. They were heroic. And they got done in an hour or so with all their buddies helping out.

Their brother, Jesse, joined in with them, too. So I got them pizza and cokes again and they ate, locked up the building and quietly left. That is the spirit of this parish. It amazes me and really makes me proud."

The new family center with a badly-needed social hall and four new classrooms, along with bathrooms with showers for future retreats, was finished in early 2003. Then renovation on the Old St. Thomas School was begun. In this building classrooms were renovated and new bathrooms were installed.

"It makes me proud to renovate this old building. It is such a part of history and now it is upgraded and made useful for a long time into the future," Father Farrell said. Sister Dorothy's Garden was revamped for the project and new areas of grass, bushes and trees were added. A large new parking lot was built to accommodate the growing parish.

The history of Sacred Heart Parish continues to be written. It is a daunting task to write such a document knowing that writing history is many times piecing together facts and figures without having the opportunity of knowing most of the people who are a part of the history, not being able to speak to them. Peoples' memories fade over time and those earliest of pioneers in the building of this parish are long gone. But we must not forget the lay people, the priests, the Sisters — all the people who have gone before us. Isn't it the Lord Jesus Christ who says, "Do this in remembrance of me"? He has asked us to not only remember, but to make history come alive.

As I sit in the church praying many a day, I sometimes can hear footsteps. I hear a door open or close and I look and no one is there. It is not a scarey feeling. It is not disconcerting. I smile to myself because I think perhaps it is Father Garnier checking on what his brave and valiant missionary efforts over a century ago has brought to fruition. Perhaps it is one of the blessed souls making a special visit, I think. One of the mothers or fathers praying for a child. Perhaps it is one of the St. Thomas children coming to peek into the cool interior. I think of Father Albert, Father Fintan, the Ursuline Sisters, Father Theophil, Father Kenneth, the families who have come here who we can assuredly say are with our

Lord in heaven having been true to Christ and to His Church. The parade of saints who have walked through these doors long before us! What a part of history we all are.

Let us remember them all, though we will not know them perhaps, till we join them in heaven one day. All the footsteps trod in Faith before us as they entered to worship our Lord at Mass on Sundays, even weekdays. All the prayers said with tears of sadness or tears of joy and thanksgiving. The hearts that have been filled with peace over these many years. Those prayers are still with us. And we continue to pray. . .

A Guided Tour:
Sacred Heart Catholic Church,
Farmington, New Mexico
By
Father Timothy Farrell, Pastor

Welcome to Sacred Heart Catholic Church and this self-guided tour. We begin on the exterior of the Church, standing in the courtyard between the church and the old parish center complex. Both of these buildings were originally built in 1929. The church building itself is a combination of brick due to the various renovations and additions over its history.

The best example of the original brick from 1929 can be found in the towers of the church. This brick, manufactured in Gallup, was used on the original building. The second major renovation, in the 1970s, can be found in the area of the sanctuary of the church, the walls nearest the rectory. The vestibule of the church which houses the stained glass windows of the Sacred Heart, Our Lady of Guadalupe and Francis of Assisi is from an addition done in the 1980s. Finally, the largest part of the brick structure was done in the major renovation in 2001.

As you stand in the courtyard, look up at the gables which were added in the 2001 renovation. These gables were used by the architects Tim Christensen and Rick Bennett to break up the very large roof needed in this renovation. In the center, large gables on both the east and west sides you will see a circle with a cross in its interior. This design was put forth by Mr. Christensen after his visit to Rome and many of the Roman Catholic churches he visited there.

The Pieta statue is a replica of the orginal brilliant work done in marble by Michelangelo. That statue is on view at St. Peter's Basilica at the Vatican.

You will note that there is a combination of reddish and yellowish brick used throughout this construction. This was to follow the original building's design.

Note the original towers from 1929. As far as is known, these are the original towers with few or no adjustments over all the years. Prior to the 2001 renovation, it was known that there was a troublesome leak in the cupola sections of the towers and this had caused major damage to the ceilings in the church. When renovation in 2001 occurred, a white metal was placed over the original material, but this did not work. Next, it was decided that the domes would be stuccoed, which would bring about a look of the Spanish Southwest. All other parts of the towers were kept as they were originally, down to the original bell from 1929, which you can hear ring only on Sunday five minutes before each Mass. All the other bells (tubular) were placed in the towers in the mid-1990s. All the bells, including the 1929 bell, are now operated electronically.

If you round the building to the Allen Avenue side nearest the tower, you will see the original cornerstone (which simply reads: "Sacred Heart 1929") stating that this church was built in 1929. Allen Avenue, it was determined at the 2001 renovation through city documents, was actually a street beside the church

many years ago. Notice the strange jog in Allen Avenue south of the church and you can note that the street originally ended right at the church. At a later point the city added a section of Allen Avenue and thus it passes slightly to the west of the original avenue.

Now we will enter the large brass doors which were added to the church when the vestibule was added in the 1980s. Donation plaques are on each door. Going through the Allen Avenue brass doors, you now enter the vestibule section built in the 1980s. Note the difference in brick from the 1929 to your left and the brick from the 1980s addition. This vestibule extended as far as the Holy Family Window. The 2001 renovation extended the vestibule to its present length and added more stained glass windows and bathrooms.

The architects decided that this vestibule could be a beautiful entrance, a hallway representing various important figures of our Faith. So standing at the brass doors and looking to your right, you will see stained glass windows placed in the church in the 1980s. First is Our Lady of Guadalupe who appeared to St. Juan Diego in the 1500s in Mexico. The image of Our Lady appeared on St. Juan Diego's tilma or

cloak and that image is still on view today at the Shrine to Our Lady of Guadalupe in Mexico City.

Next is an intriguing window of Jesus. Some state that this is his Ascension, which would seem logical, but some also state that this window also includes His Sacred Heart, due to the diamond shaped red section on his chest. Included in this image are his wounds. Around the image of Christ are important additions peculiar to our area: Sacred Heart Church itself, the oil and gas industry, the Zia symbol and an apple tree, representing the orchards which used to thrive all over the San Juan Basin.

The next window is of St. Francis of Assisi, representing the Franciscans who took over Sacred Heart Catholic Church in 1910 and who built the original church on this hill in 1929. In the window

dedicated to St. Francis, you have the Church in Assisi dedicated to the great saint, doves which represent his commitment to peace, the stigmata which Francis received as a gift from God and as a sign of his holiness, the cord with three knots standing for poverty, chastity and obedience. Note that all true images of St. Francis of Assisi have him wearing a beard.

Continuing on through the vestibule,

you will note the 2001 stained glass windows beginning with the Holy Family: Jesus, Mary and Joseph.

Next is the window of St. Angela Merici, shown teaching little children. St. Angela is the foundress of the Ursuline Sisters who taught in Sacred

Heart Parish for many decades.

Next in line is St. John Vianney, shown praying the rosary. He is the patron saint of pastors, but also is revered by diocesan priests, who founded Sacred Heart Parish in the early part of the 20th Century before handing it over to the Franciscans, and who came back to the parish when the Franciscans asked to be relieved of the duties of the parish in 1995.

Finally is St. Agnes, shown holding fire, a sign of her great holiness. Also in the window are symbols of the palm (for her martyrdom) and the lamb (Agnes means lamb). The Sisters of St. Agnes have served Sacred Heart Parish over several years now with Sister Rene Backe the last of the sisters to serve the parish before she had to leave for a

position with her congregation.

Above the doorways of each end of the vestibule are simple but beautiful stained glass windows: on the east end is a chalice with grapes, denoting the holy eucharist; on the west end is a depiction of the Holy Spirit, the dove.

Turning toward the north wall of the vestibule, in the center, you will see a crucifix of quite elaborate design. This was carved in 1947 by Rev. Timothy Brockmann, O.F.M., and is hung on the wall of what used to be part of the original 1929 lower tower. As a matter of fact, the white wall behind the crucifix was a stained glass window which had to be moved during renovation. The crucifix, relocated from the old parish center, has a beautiful corpus of Jesus hanging upon a hand-carved and hand-painted cross. Father Brockmann's

father, Herman, was a sculptor from Cincinnati and was an inspiration to his son. Father Brockmann studied drawing and clay modeling in the Cincinnati Art Academy. He exercised his skill as a cleric before ordination in the monastery of the Holy Family in Oldenburg, Indiana, where the Good Shepherd made by him welcomes you as you enter the refectory.

Best known of Father Brockmann's works is the Eucharistic Cross, which is basically what this depiction in Sacred Heart Church, is. He made more than thirty of these crosses over the years. Like much of his work, these crosses are rich in symbolism. Among the symbols on the cross in the monastery are the Franciscan coat of arms; the pelican feeding its young with its own blood, a symbol of Christ found in the catacombs; the lamb, with the chalice of the Holy Eucharist; and the inscription I H S with a halo and surrounded by flames.

The last symbol was used by St. Bernadin, a Franciscan of the 15th Century, who made the devotion to the Holy Name so popular. Also worked into the wood of the cross is a representation of the vine and the branches symbol used by Christ in referring to Himself and His followers.

Now we come to the doors from the vestibule into the main body of the church. Please note that the large windows on each side of the door have within them large wooden crosses. Actually, when the woodworkers originally put the windows in, they accidentally put them in upside down. But they liked the cross effect so much they asked if they could keep them this way. It was decided to leave the windows upside down for this reason.

Above the door and windows are three dramatic pastoral paintings done by Shiprock artist James Joe.

Originally, these paintings were not planned. But when the spaces above the windows and door were cleared, it was found that all a person could see above them was part of the floor of the choir loft, which cut across the entire space. The choir loft was built approximately seven years after the 1929 structure and it actually was built lower than it should have been.

When the three half-circle spaces were uncovered, it was determined that the Holy Trinity should be depicted in these three eyesores. Joe painted the scenery he knows well from this area. But he states that the scenery is actually his imagination striving to depict the three Persons of the Holy Trinity. At the center is God the Father, depicted by the mountain at the painting's center. A strange, yellowish glow seems to be shining through the clouds, the creative power of the Father. Note in this center section the beautiful lake, which stands for life and the goodness of God, all the greenery surrounding the mountain. Even a deer feeds near this awesome scene of creation. To the left of this painting is Joe's depiction of God the Son. The artist decided that he would not show the figure of Christ, but rather would show his footprints walking among his sheep. All the sheep seem to be feeding here and moving toward the Father. When the painting was hung in the vestibule, Joe decided he would paint a prairie dog, so common in this area. Finally, God the Holy Spirit is depicted by the rain showers, reminding us of baptism. There is a beautiful rainbow which shows the covenant between God and man. The evergreen trees are a sign of eternal life in God. And Joe painted a dove, a symbol of the Holy Spirit, just about to light upon the evergreen tree. When taken as a whole, the three paintings are actually one continuous scene, not three separate paintings. This is to embody one of the great mysteries of our Faith, that there are three distinct Persons in the One God.

Now we enter the main body of the church. You are now under the mid-1930s addition: the choir loft. In the midst of the 2001 renovation, it was found that even this addition had an addition. The front part of the choir loft had been an extension at some point and was covered in rather light plywood. It is a wonder that this did not break

under the weight of the pews and people over the many years. Now it is securely reinforced with thick floorboard and is safe for all to use.

The columns under the choir loft are from the mid-1930s, but the columns closest to the entrance are hard plastic columns painted to match the original wood columns. The contractors state that the hard plastic columns are actually stronger than the orginal columns.

If you move forward so that you are standing out from under the choir loft, look up at the vaulted celing. Imagine the 1929 orginal church. Its walls ended at the present columns on both sides. The choir loft was not yet built. The seam you see in the vaulted celing is where the altar used to be. That was the original size of the church! You can now understand why Father Kenneth Robertson, O.F.M., in the 1970s, extended the church northward and replicated the 1929 altar area.

The ten stained-glass windows to your right and left in the main body of the Church (in the area of the pews) are all depicting the life of Jesus. They were commissioned in 1999 and made by Potente Studios in association with Jaeger Studios, both in Wisconsin.

From the front left to the back left, they depict: The Annunciation; The Nativity of Our Lord; The Baptism of Jesus; The Good Shepherd; The Last Supper.

From back right to front right: The Agony in the Garden;

The Crucifixion; The Resurrection; The Ascension; and Pentecost.

Also commissioned that same year were the two windows in the balcony area: The Sacred Heart of Jesus and the Immaculate Heart of Mary. In the stairwell of the church is the window depicting Hope. The other windows depicting the virtues Faith and Love are in the meditation room at the far end of the balcony in the bell tower section.

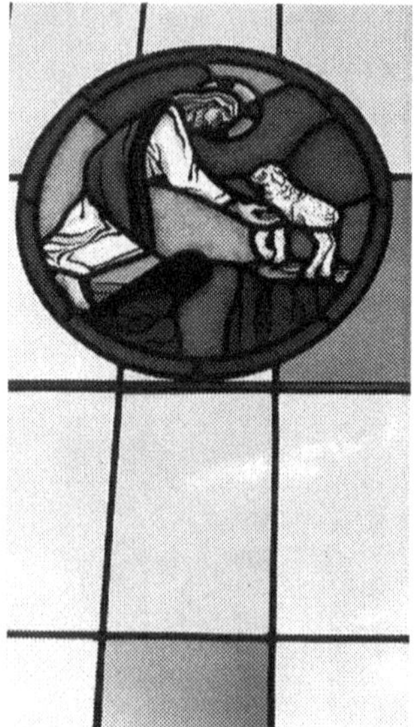

The final two windows placed in the church in 1999 were in the Confessional. The windows are Jesus Seeking the Lost Sheep and the Prodigal Son.

The windows in the Cry Room are newly made and placed in 2001. They depict Jesus and the Little Children and Blessed Kateri Tekakwitha.

The windows which were replaced by the stained glass were hard plastic with a brown cross surrounded by a deep yellow. These windows were donated to Christ the

King Parish and now cover the windows in the old parish church in Shiprock.

At the center of the altar area, on either side of the Tabernacle, are two of the oldest items in the church, which stained glass window experts believe are dated between 1900 and 1910. It is not

certain if these windows came from the original structure where Drake Drilling is now operating. In the photos of the church, there is no indication of any stained-glass windows. These windows are actually not stained glass but rather painted glass windows.

One depicts the Cross of Christ with a wreath of the Crown of Thorns around the Cross. The other depicts the Lamb of God, Jesus, carrying the banner of Easter: the white flag with the red cross.

In the Sanctuary area are six new sacrament windows. The three on the left, looking towards the altar, are Baptism, Reconciliation and Confirmation. On the right of the altar area are three more: Holy Matrimony,

Holy Orders and Anointing of the Sick. The Holy Eucharist is present in the Church in the Tabernacle, so there was no need for a window for the Eucharist.

The small, dark wooden crosses on four parts of the inner church are made by Joe Vinzenz and designate the places blessed by Most Rev. Donald Pelotte, third bishop of Gallup, when he rededicated the church and

HOLY OIL
IN LOVING MEMORY

JESUS IS CONDEMNED TO DEATH

blessed the altar on October 25th, 2001.

The Stations of the Cross date from 1935, when Father Roger Henehold, O.F.M., served as pastor. They represent 14 scenes in the history of our Lord's passion and death. They were donated to the church by Mr. T. Vincent Shannon in memory of his mother, Mrs. Agnes Ellen Shannon. The stations were made by the Daprato Statuary Company of Boston, Massachusetts.

The statues of St. Francis of Assisi and St. Anthony of Padua

seem to have come from the earliest days of the Franciscans entrance into this area. They appear in the earliest photos, at least, from 1929. The statues of the Sacred Heart of Jesus and the Immaculate Heart of Mary, though, appear to be from a later date because they replace earlier statues of the same subject matter which appear in the earliest photographs of the 1929 church. St. Joseph and the Child Jesus and St. Therese of Liseux are near the vestibule entrance. St.

Therese is in most churches in the Diocese of Gallup because she is the patroness of mission churches and the Diocese of Gallup is a mission diocese.

The inner two rows of pews are from the renovation and extension of the church in the 1970s under the leadership of Father Kenneth Robertson. The new pews in both the left and the right sections of the 2001 renovations are solid wood made by the Trinity Furniture Company in Trinity, Texas. The new pews came already padded, but the old pews were re-upholstered here in the church in the 2001 renovation.

Blue carpeting and blue cusions adorn the church and Al Newton and his co-workers painted the church a light rose color in the interior and re-stained all the wood in the interior. They also painted the exterior trim and all the areas on the church towers.

Insulation was done by Valencia Insulation, including a large insulating project in the great vaulted ceiling which had never been done before and this went a long way towards saving energy.

All stained glass windows and all the pews were dedicated by parishioners and plaques were placed on each of the dedicated items throughout the church, including the meditation room, the painting of the Holy Trinity, and the door and window work in the vestibule.

Before we close our tour of Sacred Heart Church, let us note two very important final items in the church. One is the baptismal font to the left of the altar in the alcove surrounded by the Baptismal, Confessional and Confirmation windows. This baptismal font was found in the basement of the church during the renovation. It was refurbished and redesigned by Robert Childers, a member of the parish. He had a blue bowl hand made by a Durango artist placed in its interior.

Also, the small cabinet near the baptismal font was made by Jerry Nix, a local woods craftsman. Please note the shell design on the exterior. The shell is one of the symbols of baptism, as you will note in the window nearby.

The final piece to note is the "gifts table." This table was given by the Shannon Family, one of the early pioneer families of the area who were founding members of the parish. The table is from the 1920s and was in the original church located on Pinon Street.

Franciscan Roster

1910— Fintan Zumbahien, O.F.M.
1910— Albertus Daeger, O.F.M.
1911— Theodor Stephan, O.F.M.
1912— Felician Sandford, O.F.M.
1920— Celsus Koenig, O.F.M.
1921— Camillus Fangmann, O.F.M.
1921— Titus Qehring, O.F.M.
1922—Sixtus Kopp, O.F.M.
1922—Aloysius Albrecht, O.F.M.
1924—Marcellus Troester, O.F.M.
1924—Barnabas Meyer, O.F.M.
1924—Benedict Noellers, O.F.M.
1928—Theodosius Meyer, O.F.M.
1931—Clementine Wottle, O.F.M.
1931—Donald Herp, O.F.M.
1934—Pax Schicker, O.F.M.
1934—Eusebius Schweitzer, O.F.M.
1935— Roger Hengehold O.F.M.
1935— Celestine Matz, O.F.M.
1939— Theophil Meyer, O.F.M.
1940— Michael Ziegler, O.F.M.
1942— Florentine Meyers, O.F.M.
1942— Edward Leary, O.F.M.
1943— Blase Brickweg, O.F.M.
1943— Thomas Blomstrom, O.F.M.
1944— Anthony Kroger, O.F.M.
1945—Alexius Wecker, O.F.M.
1948— Pacian Meyer, O.F.M.
1953— Pius Winter, O.F.M.
1955— Finnian Connolly, O.F.M.
1957 — Reynaldo Rivera, O.F.M.

1957 — Kenneth Robertson, O.F.M.
1958 — Conran Runnebaum, O.F.M.
1961 — Harold Geers, O.F.M.
1961 — Godfrey Blank, O.F.M.
1964 — Neri Greskoviak, O.F.M.
1964 — Gerard H. Geier, O.F.M.
1966 — Raymond Soper, O.F.M.
1966 — Ronnin G. Einhaus, O.F.M.
1969 — Timon Cook, O.F.M.
1969 — Herman Harkins, O.F.M.
1970 — Dennet Jung, O.F.M.
1971 — Joseph Zink, O.F.M.
1972 — Emmeran Frank, O.F.M.
1974 — Benedict Begin, O.F.M.
1977 — Dan Havron, O.F.M.
1977 — Antonio Valdez, O.F.M.
1978 — Casey Kolesar, O.F.M.
1979 — Roy Effler, O.F.M.
1980 — Brian Morrow, O.F.M.
1981 — Dacian Batt, O.F.M.
1982 — Ivo Zirkelbach, O.F.M.
1982 — John Lanzrath, O.F.M.
1984 — Valentine Young, O.F.M.
1986 — Lawrence Schreiber, O.F.M.

The final Franciscans to man Sacred Heart were Father Meldon Hickey, O.F.M., as pastor, and Father Paul Juniet as associate. They left in September, 1995.

Ursuline Roster

S. Margaret Mary Barrow 1919-1940; 1944-1950

S. Antionette Krampe 1919-1923

S. Veronica Benedict 1919-1922

S. Edmund Coomes 1922-1924

S. George Marie Morgan 1923-1926

S. Dorothy Payne 1924-1969; ret. 1976-1979

S. Pierre Brady 1928-193 1; 1945-46

S. James Alma Bickeft 1930-193 6

S. Frances Xavier Miles 1931-1933

S. Angelina Payne 1933-1934

S. Marie Therese Brumlow 1934-1936

S. M. Magdalene Barrett 1936-1938

S. Mary Martin Sisk 1936-1941

S. Charles Marie Coyle 1936-1943

S. Rosita Willett 194 1-1945

S. Annunciata Durr 1941-1943

S. Francis Borgia Wathen 1943-1950

S. Mary Benigna (Naomi) Aull 1945-1948

S. Mary Regis Ramold 1946-47

S. Joseph Cecilia Muller 1947-1950

S. Bartholene Warren 1948-1950; 1970-1976

S. Elizabeth Ann Ray 1950-1956

S. Charles Albert Rowe 1950-1952

S. Ancilla Marie Warren 1950-1955; 1962-1980; 1981-88;
1983-1988(Lived there as Diocesan Music Supr.)

S. Louis Marie (Luisa) Bickett 1950-1961

S. Mary Jane Hicks 1952-1960

S. Francis Mary Wilhelm 1952-1961

S. Frances Ursula Heimes Dec. 1952-1953

S. Joseph Raymond Payne 1953-1961

S. Mary Xavier Trujillo 1954-1956

S. Georgetta Higdon 1955-March 1957

S. Marie Montgomery 1956-1958; 1973-1991
S. Margaret Joseph Aull 1956-1967
S.Robert Mary Kennedy 1957-1958
S. Edwina Barrow 1958-1963.
S. Marie Brenda Vowels 1958-1959
S. Peter Claver Abell 1958-1962
S. Mary Serra Goethals 1958-1959
S. Isabel Beavin 1959-1963
S. Charles Catherine Medley 1959-1962
S. Rose Lima Head 1960-1965
S. Mary Savio Garcia 1961-1966
S. Marie Secunda Mudd 1962-1965
S. Joseph Adrian Russell 1962-1964
S. Vincent Mary Pryor 1962-1966
S. Mary Henry Russell 1963-1966
S. Mary Jovita Milner 1964-1970
S. Joseph Alice Johnson 1965-1971
S. Virginia Mary Nichols 1965-1974
S. Robert Ann Wheatley 1965-1967
S. Jean Richard Stukenholtz 1966-1971
S. Margaret Ann Wathen 1967-1974
S. Francis Louise Johnson 1967-1970
S. Angela Marie Krampe 1969-70
S. Bartholene Warren 1970-1976
S. Rose Carrico 1970-1972
S. Alice Mayo 1971-72
S. Mary Clement Greenwell 1972-73
S. Michael Ann Monaghan 1972-1977
S. Sara Marie Gomez 1972-73 (also served in the late 1990s and early 2000s)
S. Mary Evelyn Duvall 1973-1996
S. Jean Bernadine Collard 1974-75
S. Charles Marie Coyle 1975-1981
S. Praxedes Spalding 1977-78

END NOTE

This history was compiled from diocesan resources, as well as "A Brief History of Sacred Heart Parish Farmington 1905-1987" by Father Dacian Batt, O.F.M. and "Candles of the Lord" by the Ursuline Sisters.